I0410796

CONTENTS

OBJECTIVES AND METHODOLOGY..1

BACKGROUND 2

THE DEPARTMENT DOES NOT CONSISTENTLY MEET FOIA LEGAL AND REGULATORY
REQUIREMENTS...6

    Statutory Deadlines for Processing Requests Are Not Met...6

    S/ES Does Not Routinely Follow Requirements To Search Email.......................................8

PROCEDURAL WEAKNESSES CONTRIBUTE TO DEFICIENT FOIA SEARCHES AND RESPONSES.....10

    Current S/ES FOIA Processes Are Inadequate...10

    S/ES FOIA Searches and Responses Are Sometimes Inaccurate and Incomplete........................13

RECOMMENDATIONS..16

APPENDIX A: MANAGEMENT RESPONSES...18

ABBREVIATIONS 24

OIG EVALUATIONS AND SPECIAL PROJECTS TEAM...25

OBJECTIVES AND METHODOLOGY

In April 2015, the Office of Inspector General (OIG) initiated an evaluation to address concerns identified during recent audits and inspections[1] and to respond to requests from the current Secretary of State and several Members of Congress involving a variety of issues, including the use of non-Departmental systems[2] to conduct official business, records preservation requirements, and Freedom of Information Act (FOIA) compliance. This report, which is one of several documenting OIG's findings in these areas, addresses efforts undertaken by the Department of State (Department) to ensure that government records are properly produced in response to FOIA requests involving past and current Secretaries of State. Specifically, this report assesses (1) the Department's compliance with FOIA statutory and regulatory requirements and (2) the effectiveness of the processes used by the Office of the Secretary, Executive Secretariat (S/ES), to respond to FOIA requests. OIG has already issued findings related to one aspect of the FOIA process used to review and release 55,000 pages of emails that former Secretary of State Hillary Rodham Clinton provided to the Department in December 2014.[3] OIG will report separately on issues associated with the use of non-Departmental systems to conduct official business and records preservation requirements.

In planning this work, OIG drew on FOIA, and related regulations and guidance issued by the Department, and *Standards for Internal Control in the Federal Government*.[4] To gain an understanding of the Department's FOIA processes, controls, and policies and procedures, OIG interviewed the Under Secretary for Management, the Assistant Secretary for the Bureau of

---

[1] OIG has identified the following issues: inconsistencies across the Department in identifying and preserving records, hacking incidents and other issues affecting the security of Department electronic communication, delays and other problems related to processing FOIA requests, and concerns about an Ambassador's use of private email to conduct official business. *See* OIG, *Review of State Messaging and Archive Retrieval Toolset and Record Email* (ISP-I-15-15, March 2015); OIG, *Audit of the Department of State Information Security Program* (AUD-IT-15-17, October 2014); OIG, *Management Alert: OIG Findings of Significant and Recurring Weaknesses in the Department of State Information System Security Program* (AUD-IT-14-04, November 2013); OIG, *Inspection of the Bureau of Administration, Global Information Services, Office of Information Programs and Services* (ISP-I-12-54, September 2012); and OIG, *Inspection of Embassy Nairobi, Kenya* (ISP-I-12-38A, August 2012).

[2] For purposes of this work, OIG uses the term "non-Departmental systems" to mean hardware and software that is not owned, provided, monitored, or certified by the Department of State.

[3] OIG, *Potential Issues Identified by the Office of the Inspector General of the Intelligence Community Concerning the Department of State's Process for the Review of Former Secretary Clinton's Emails under the Freedom of Information Act* (ESP-15-04, July 17, 2015). This report made four recommendations to strengthen the Department's review of records prior to release: (1) requesting staff support from intelligence community FOIA offices to assist in the identification of IC equities, (2) facilitating a review of records by IC FOIA officials to ensure that the Department's Classified Network is appropriate for storage of FOIA material, (3) seeking classification expertise from the interagency to act as a final arbiter if there is a question regarding potentially classified material, and (4) incorporating the Department of Justice into the FOIA process to ensure the legal sufficiency review of the FOIA exemptions and redactions. In response, the Department agreed with recommendations 1 and 4, but did not agree with recommendations 2 and 3.

[4] Government Accountability Office (GAO), *Standards for Internal Control in the Federal Government* (GAO-14-704G, September 2014).

Administration (A), and various officials in the Office of Global Information Services (A/GIS) and S/ES. In addition, OIG reviewed the Department's annual FOIA reports and obtained and analyzed a list of all FOIA requests tasked to the Office of the Secretary from 1996 to 2015. OIG also consulted with the National Archives and Records Administration's Office of Government Information Services and reviewed the FOIA procedures of other Federal agencies. OIG conducted this work in accordance with quality standards for evaluations as set forth by the Council of the Inspectors General on Integrity and Efficiency.

BACKGROUND

Enacted in 1966, FOIA provides that any person has a right, enforceable in court, to obtain access to Federal agency records, except to the extent that such records (or portions of them) are protected from public disclosure by one of the Act's exemptions or exclusions.[5] The Act defines "record" broadly and covers "any information that would be an agency record subject to the requirements of [FOIA] when maintained by an agency in any format, including an electronic format."[6]

Upon receipt of a request for records, the agency is required to determine whether to comply and to notify the requester of its determination and the justification for it within 20 working days.[7] The notification of an adverse determination could be a denial of the request in whole or in part based on the statutory exemptions or a determination that no such records exist. The exemptions include, for example, classified information, privileged communications, and law enforcement information.[8]

In an adverse determination, the agency must notify the requester that he or she has a right to appeal the determination to the head of the agency. An administrative appeal shall be decided within 20 working days.[9] If the appeal is not favorable, the requester may then file a complaint in Federal district court to enjoin the agency from withholding agency records and to order the

---

[5] FOIA, 5 U.S.C. § 552. If an exemption applies, the agency must notify the requester that a record exists but is exempt from disclosure. If an exclusion applies, the agency may notify the requester that no responsive records subject to FOIA exist. Exclusions relate to the existence of an ongoing criminal investigation, the names of informants, and classified foreign intelligence or counterintelligence or international terrorism records.

[6] 5 U.S.C. § 552(f)(2)(A).

[7] 5 U.S.C. § 552(a)(6)(A)(i). In unusual circumstances, the time limit for responding to a request or an appeal may be extended by up to ten working days. 5 U.S.C. § 552(a)(6)(B).

[8] 5 U.S.C. § 552(b).The nine exemptions are (1) information that is classified to protect national security, (2) information related solely to the internal personnel rules and practices of an agency, (3) information that is prohibited from disclosure by another Federal law, (4) trade secrets or commercial or financial information that is confidential or privileged, (5) privileged communications within or between agencies, (6) information that if disclosed would unwarrantedly invade another individual's personal privacy, (7) certain information compiled for law enforcement purposes, (8) information that concerns the supervision of financial institutions, and (9) geological information on wells.

[9] 5 U.S.C. § 552(a)(6)(A). This includes a determination that no responsive records exist.

---

production of any agency records the requester believes the agency improperly withheld.[10] In addition, a requester who receives no response within 20 days has a right to file a complaint in district court immediately.[11]

At the Department, the *Foreign Affairs Manual* (FAM) designates the Office of Information Programs and Services (IPS) as responsible for the Department's compliance with FOIA.[12] IPS is a part of the Office of Global Information Services, a subcomponent of the Bureau of Administration. The FAM also designates the Assistant Secretary for Administration as the Chief FOIA Officer, responsible for Department-wide FOIA compliance.[13] The Assistant Secretary for Administration reports to the Under Secretary for Management.[14]

IPS administers the Department's Information Access Program, which includes administering all requests for FOIA records. IPS coordinates, tracks, and reports on responses to all FOIA requests for Department records—including administrative appeals made in connection with such requests—and is supposed to ensure that responses are timely, accurate, and complete.[15] The Department's FOIA regulations specify that FOIA requests be sent to IPS.[16] The request must reasonably describe the records sought, should be specific, and should include all pertinent details about the request, including the subject, timeframe, any individuals involved, and reasons why the Department is believed to have records on the subject of the request.[17]

Once a FOIA request is received, IPS logs it into the case-tracking system—the Freedom of Information Document Management System (FREEDOMS)—and acknowledges the request. IPS then determines which Department bureaus, offices, or overseas posts would possess the requested records and sends a search/review request transmittal (Form DS-1748) to each office FOIA coordinator. The form requires each office to provide information on the files searched and their location, the search terms used, and the time period searched, among other information.

In 2010, the Department issued guidance to offices that describes in general terms how a search is to take place.

> Offices must undertake searches that are reasonably calculated to uncover all
> relevant materials. Unless otherwise noted in a given request, offices should
> conduct a search for records in any form, including paper records, email

---

[10] 5 U.S.C. § 552(a)(4)(B). As an alternative to litigation, a requester may request mediation with the agency, which is conducted by the Office of Government Information Services in the National Archives and Records Administration. 5 U.S.C. § 552(h)(3).

[11] 5 U.S.C. § 552 (a)(6)(C)(i).

[12] 1 FAM 214.2.

[13] 1 FAM 211.2(ee). Executive Order 13392 requires the designation of a Chief FOIA Officer.

[14] 1 FAM 211.2(a)

[15] U.S. Department of State, *FOIA Guidance For State Department Employees* (2010), at 3.

[16] 22 C.F.R. § 171.5(a).

[17] 22 C.F.R. § 171.5(c).

(including email in personal folders and attachments to email), and other electronic records on servers, on workstations, or in Department databases. Offices do not, however, need to search where there is no reasonable possibility of finding responsive records.[18]

Once the search office returns responsive records to IPS, IPS determines their relevance to the request and whether any part of them may be released to the requester or whether they are subject to one of FOIA's exemptions.[19] IPS then prepares the formal response to the requester and includes any responsive records that are subject to release. If a requester files an administrative appeal of an adverse determination, it is adjudicated by the Appeals Review Panel, consisting of retired Foreign Service Officers.[20]

---

[18] *FOIA Guidance For State Department Employees,* at 8.

[19] Certain offices, including the Bureau of Diplomatic Security and the Office of Medical Services, are referred to as "decentralized offices" and review their own documents for exemptions. However, these offices must still forward a copy of their response to the request to IPS.

[20] 22 C.F.R. § 171.52.

Figure 1: FOIA Process for Requests Involving the Office of the Secretary

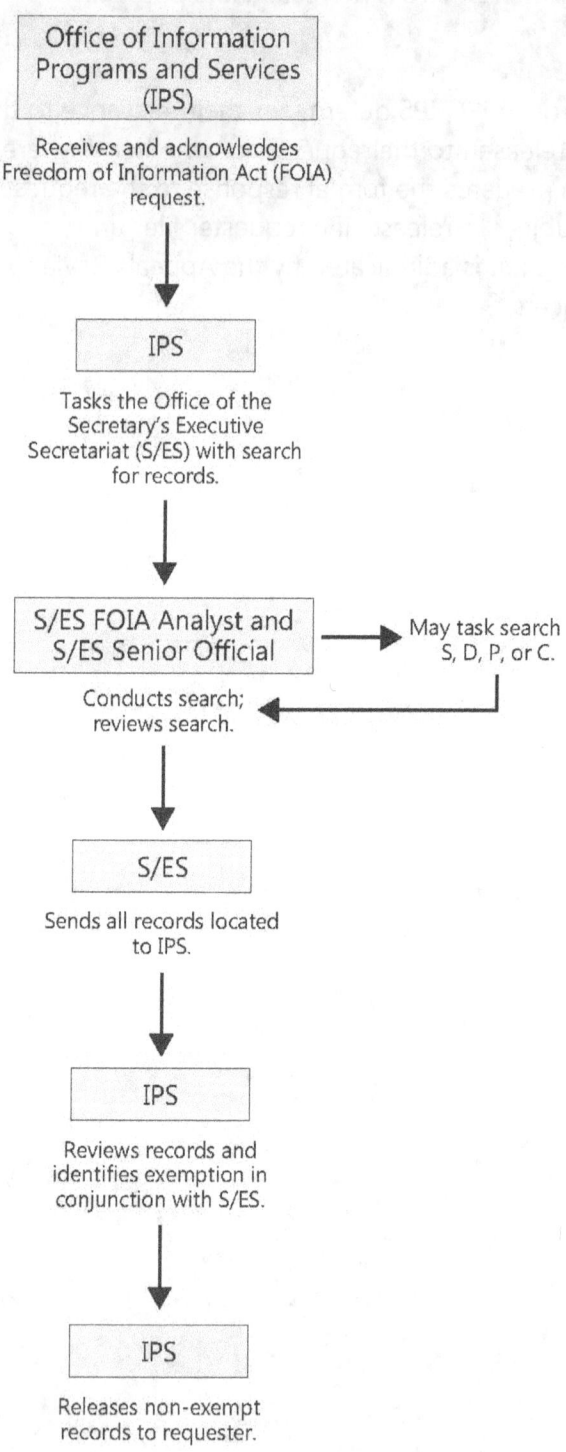

Office of Information Programs and Services (IPS)

Receives and acknowledges Freedom of Information Act (FOIA) request.

IPS

Tasks the Office of the Secretary's Executive Secretariat (S/ES) with search for records.

S/ES FOIA Analyst and S/ES Senior Official

May task search to S, D, P, or C.

Conducts search; reviews search.

S/ES

Sends all records located to IPS.

IPS

Reviews records and identifies exemption in conjunction with S/ES.

IPS

Releases non-exempt records to requester.

As shown in Figure 1, when a FOIA request involves documents produced by a Secretary of State or other officials in the Office of the Secretary (S), the two Deputy Secretaries of State (D), the Under Secretary for Political Affairs (P), or the Counselor of the Department (C), IPS tasks S/ES with performing a search for relevant documents. S/ES is responsible for the coordination of material presented to the Secretary, Deputy Secretary, and Under Secretaries; the implementation of decisions made by these officials; and the Department's relations with the White House, National Security Council, and other Cabinet agencies.[21] S/ES employs one FOIA Analyst, who reports to the GS-14 Deputy Director of Correspondence, Records, & Staffing (Deputy Director).[22] The Deputy Director serves as the S/ES FOIA coordinator and reports to the Director of Secretariat Staff.

According to information provided by S/ES, the FOIA Analyst searches for relevant documents in several databases or tasks the relevant office (S, D, P, or C) with performing the search. After the search is completed, the Deputy Director conducts a review of the FOIA Analyst's search and the records identified. Finally, all identified records are sent to IPS for processing, along with a signed form DS-1748 identifying the databases searched and the time expended in conducting the search. If the request is in litigation or if legal guidance is sought regarding the search, an attorney from the Office of the Legal Adviser (L) may review the proposed response before it is released to the requester.

---

[21] 1 FAM 022.2.

[22] A second S/ES employee occasionally assists with FOIA searches in addition to his regular duties.

In September 2015, Secretary of State John Kerry named a former career Senior Foreign Service Officer as the Department's Transparency Coordinator. The Transparency Coordinator will lead the Department's efforts to meet the President's *Managing Government Records* directive, respond to OIG's recommendations, and work with other agencies and the private sector to explore best practices and new technologies. Secretary Kerry also tasked the Transparency Coordinator with improving the efficiency of the Department's systems for responding to FOIA and congressional requests.

THE DEPARTMENT DOES NOT CONSISTENTLY MEET FOIA LEGAL AND REGULATORY REQUIREMENTS

Statutory Deadlines for Processing Requests Are Not Met

FOIA requires agencies to respond to FOIA requests within 20 working days. However, the Department rarely meets this statutory deadline, even for simple requests. Although few agencies are able to meet the 20-day deadline for complex requests,[23] overall compliance is much greater across the Federal Government than at the Department. In FY 2014, the average processing time for simple requests across the Federal Government was 20.5 days, and the Government-wide average for complex requests was slightly less than 119 days.[24] In contrast, the Department took four and one-half times as long—an average of 91 days to process simple requests and almost 535 days to process complex requests.[25]

The Department has been particularly late in meeting FOIA's timelines for requests involving the Office of the Secretary. Table 1, which is based on IPS data provided to OIG, shows the processing time for FOIA requests that were tasked to S/ES and involved the current and past

---

[23] The Department of Justice, which is required by FOIA to develop reporting and performance guidelines, defines a complex request as one that involves a high volume of material or requires additional steps to process, such as the need to search for records in multiple locations. An example of a simple request is a single individual's visa record. An example of a complex request is one for all records relating to the attacks on U.S. diplomatic facilities in Benghazi, Libya, which covers multiple bureaus and offices of the Department. *See* U.S. Department of Justice, *Guide to the Freedom of Information Act* (2009).

[24] U.S. Department of Justice, *Summary of Annual FOIA Reports For Fiscal Year 2014*, pp. 12–14.

[25] U.S. Department of State, *Freedom of Information Act Annual Report, Fiscal Year 2014*, p. 28. In its 2015 analysis of the performance of the 15 Federal agencies that consistently receive the most FOIA requests, the Center for Effective Government rated the Department as the lowest scoring agency by far. Its analysis demonstrated that the Department processed only 17 percent of the FOIA requests it received in 2013. Center for Effective Government, *Making the Grade: Access to Information Scorecard 2015* (March 2015), p. 2. The Department's Chief FOIA Officer attributed these delays to (1) a large increase in requests and (2) an increase in complex requests. The Department's requests have increased in recent years; however, this increase in requests exists across the Federal Government and is not unique to the Department.

---

four Secretaries of State.[26] Only 14 of the 417 FOIA requests were completed within the statutory timeframe. Fifty-five of the requests took more than 500 days to process. The majority of the requests, 243 of 417, are still pending; several of these pending requests were received years ago. For example, 10 of the 23 pending requests relating to former Secretary of State Colin Powell are at least 5 years old.

Table 1: Processing Time for FOIA Requests Related to Recent Secretaries of State

| | Requests Completed Within Listed Times | | | | | |
Secretary	Up to 20 Days	21–100 Days	101–500 Days	500+ Days	Still Pending	Total Number of FOIA Requests
Albright	1	0	2	4	2	9
Powell	8	4	37	27	23	99
Rice	1	3	7	9	20	40
Clinton	3	19	27	14	177	240
Kerry	1	2	4	1	21	29
Total	14	28	77	55	243	417

Source: OIG analysis of IPS data, as of June 2015.

In 2012, OIG reported that one of the key reasons for the timeliness problem was that a relatively small number of IPS staff were processing the heavy volume of Department-wide requests.[27] Since then, as shown in Figure 2, FOIA requests have increased, yet the Department has allocated fewer employees to handle them. According to IPS, some of these employees have been assigned hundreds of requests each and face severe challenges in properly managing their caseloads.

Figure 2: IPS Staff Devoted to Processing Department-wide FOIA Requests

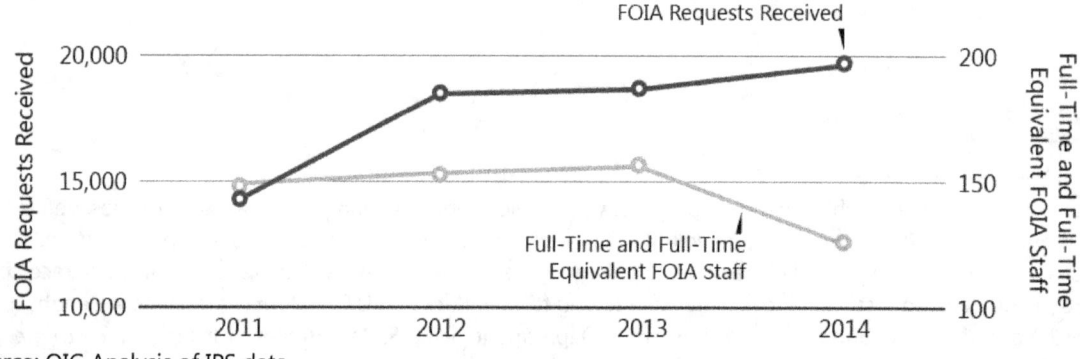

Source: OIG Analysis of IPS data.

---

[26] S/ES told OIG that its statistics differ from IPS data, but agreed to work with IPS to reconcile the inconsistencies. The FOIA process has several steps, and IPS often tasks multiple offices with responding to requests. Thus, the delays noted in this chart could have occurred at multiple steps in the process and are not necessarily attributable to S/ES search delays.

[27] OIG, *Inspection of the Bureau of Administration, Global Information Services, Office of Information Programs and Services* (ISP-I-12-54, September 2012). GAO also stressed the importance of redirecting or acquiring resources to clear backlogs in a 2012 report on FOIA compliance across the Government. *See* GAO, *Freedom of Information Act: Additional Actions Can Strengthen Agency Efforts to Improve Management* (GAO-12-828, July 2012).

Furthermore, approximately one-third of IPS staff have been assigned to work on one FOIA case in litigation, *Leopold v. Department of State*, in which the court ordered a rolling production of the approximately 55,000 pages of former Secretary Clinton's emails that she provided to the Department in December 2014, while other FOIA work is understaffed.[28]

In each of the past 3 years, IPS has attempted to address this issue by requesting additional personnel to meet the rising caseload, including its most recent request to the Bureau of Administration for 27 additional staff, which it estimated would result in a 10-percent reduction in the FOIA backlog. However, the Department has not provided any additional permanent personnel.

In late September 2015, the Under Secretary for Management decided to detail staff already within the Department to IPS. However, little progress has been made to date to resolve the personnel shortage. On September 2, 2015, the Department solicited expressions of interest from current and retired Department employees in a 9 to 12 month detail to IPS. As of the beginning of November, 7 temporary employees had started work.

S/ES Does Not Routinely Follow Requirements To Search Email

As a general rule, an agency must undertake a FOIA search that is "reasonably calculated to uncover all relevant documents."[29] Since 1997, FOIA has specified that agencies must make a reasonable effort to search for requested documents in electronic form or format, except when such efforts would "significantly interfere" with the operation of an agency's information system.[30] In 2010, the Department issued more explicit requirements for FOIA compliance:

> Unless otherwise noted in a given request, offices should conduct a search for records in any form, including paper records, email (including email in personal folders and attachments to email), and other electronic records on servers, on workstations, or in Department databases.[31]

In addition to searching paper records, S/ES typically searches for relevant documents in several electronic databases, including classified files, the Department's cable and telegram systems, the Secretariat Tracking and Retrieval System (STARS), and EVEREST (which replaced STARS).[32] None

---

[28] The Department anticipates completing the court-ordered production in January 2016.

[29] *Weisberg v. U.S. Dep't of Justice*, 705 F 2d 1344, 1351 (D.C.Cir. 1983).

[30] 5 U.S.C. § 552(a)(3)(C)).

[31] *FOIA Guidance For State Department Employees*, at 8.

[32] According to information provided by S/ES, EVEREST is a web-based application that provides the Secretary of State and other senior Department principals the ability to receive foreign policy memoranda and correspondence from Department bureaus and offices electronically, as well as task and track the paperless submission of most memoranda. Correspondence and memoranda can include internal and external letters, action memos, information memos, briefing checklists, and telephone talking points, as well as documents received from other agencies. Incoming documents are uploaded (in their native format) by originating offices into EVEREST, submitted to the Executive Secretary for review, and forwarded electronically to the relevant Department principal. EVEREST replaced

---

of these databases are intended to archive email files. STARS and EVEREST are systems used to route foreign policy memoranda and other documents to the Office of the Secretary. S/ES rarely searched electronic email accounts prior to 2011 and still does not consistently search these accounts, even when relevant records are likely to be uncovered through such a search. For example, S/ES has not searched email accounts for requests seeking all "correspondence" between the Secretary of State and another party. The FOIA Analyst described the decision to search email accounts to be a discretionary one that is only exercised periodically.

According to the Deputy Director's explanation of current practices, S/ES initiates a search of email accounts only if a FOIA request mentions emails or explicitly refers to "all records." S/ES will also search email if it is requested to do so by an L attorney during the course of litigation arising over FOIA issues. If a FOIA request specifically asks for emails of a current employee, the FOIA Analyst tasks S, D, P, or C with searching for the records but does not review the search methodology or approve the results. It appears that current S, D, P, and C employees search through their own email accounts for responsive records.[33] If the FOIA request specifically asks for emails of a former employee, the FOIA Analyst requests the applicable stored electronic file from the S/ES Office of Information Resources Management (S/ES-IRM), the office that handles information technology for the Office of the Secretary.[34] S/ES-IRM reported to OIG that it has maintained files numbering in the thousands for selected senior officials[35] dating back at least as far as Secretary Powell's tenure, though OIG has determined that many of these are not easily accessible.[36] Moreover, as the Deputy Director noted, searching these files is difficult because searches are limited to those that can be undertaken using Microsoft Outlook.[37]

FOIA neither authorizes nor requires agencies to search for Federal records in personal email accounts maintained on private servers or through commercial providers (for example, Gmail, Yahoo, and Hotmail).[38] Furthermore, the FOIA Analyst has no way to independently locate Federal records from such accounts unless employees take steps to preserve official emails in

---

STARS on January 1, 2015, and serves as a permanent, searchable record for the Secretary of State and other senior Department principals memoranda. STARS is a legacy system that was designed to manage the flow of foreign policy memoranda and correspondence both to and from the Secretary of State and other senior Department principals. Incoming and outgoing documents were scanned into STARS, manually indexed (through use of a brief abstract summarizing the substance of the document and identifying document-specific key words), and stored as document images. Searches are limited to retrieval of material based on index terms attached to the document; the document images themselves cannot be searched using text-based search methods. New entries into STARS ended January 1, 2015, but it continues to be used to locate and retrieve documents.

[33] OIG did not evaluate the practices used by S, D, P, and C.

[34] S/ES-IRM stores the files in Personal Storage Table (.pst) files, a format used to store copies of email messages, calendar events, and other items within Microsoft software.

[35] S/ES-IRM does not maintain an index or inventory of these files.

[36] In 2015, the Department began permanently retaining the emails of 102 senior officials.

[37] S/ES has begun testing software intended to enhance its ability to search and retrieve email records.

[38] Records subject to FOIA are those that are (1) either created or obtained by an agency and (2) under agency control at the time of the FOIA request. *U.S. Dept. of Justice v. Tax Analysts*, 492 U.S. 136 (1989). *See also Competitive Enter. Inst. v. Office of Sci. and Tech. Policy*, No. 14-765, 2015 WL 967549 (D.D.C. March 3, 2015).

Department recordkeeping systems. OIG will report separately on preservation requirements applicable to past and current Secretaries of State and the Department's efforts to recover Federal records from personal accounts. However, under current law and Department policy, employees who use personal email to conduct official business are required to forward or copy email from a personal account to their respective Department accounts within 20 days.[39] The Deputy Director, who has handled FOIA responsibilities for S/ES since 2006, could not recall any instances of emails from personal accounts being provided to him in response to a search tasked to an S/ES component.[40]

PROCEDURAL WEAKNESSES CONTRIBUTE TO DEFICIENT FOIA SEARCHES AND RESPONSES

Current S/ES FOIA Processes Are Inadequate

Although specific details of processes for handling FOIA requests vary among agencies, the major steps in processing a request are similar across the Federal Government. Recent assessments of the Department's processes revealed poor practices. In 2012, OIG's inspection of A/GIS found, among other deficiencies, that FOIA requests are prone to delay and that IPS lacked a sound process to develop its information systems.[41] A 2015 report by the Center for Effective Government found that, among 15 agencies that receive a large volume of public records requests, the Department ranked last, in part because of increased processing times and outdated regulations.[42] According to the report, the Department was the only agency whose rules do not require staff to notify requesters when processing is delayed, even though this is mandated by law. Furthermore, little attention has been paid to the accuracy and completeness of responses to FOIA requests. The Department has not sent out a notice or memorandum reminding employees of their FOIA responsibilities since March 2009, when former Secretary Clinton sent a message commemorating Freedom of Information Day.

Although OIG focused on procedural weaknesses in the Office of the Secretary for this evaluation, the issues OIG identified have broader implications. *Standards for Internal Control in the Federal Government* stresses that the tone at the top—management's philosophy and operating style—is fundamental to an effective internal control system.[43] OIG's past and current

---

[39] 44 U.S.C. 2911; Department of State, *A Message from Under Secretary for Management Patrick F. Kennedy regarding State Department Records Responsibilities and Policy*, Announcement No. 2014_10_115, October 17, 2014.

[40] In November 2014, the Department sent a request to former Secretaries of State for any Federal records that were housed on personal email. In March 2015, the Department sent similar requests to several staff members who worked for former Secretary Clinton. The Department has and continues to produce some of the records received from these requests in response to FOIA requests.

[41] OIG, *Inspection of the Bureau of Administration, Global Information Services, Office of Information Programs and Services* (ISP-I-12-54, September 2012).

[42] Center for Effective Government, *Making the Grade: Access to Information Scorecard 2015* (March 2015).

[43] GAO-14-704G, §§ 1.02 to 1.05.

work demonstrates that Department leadership has not played a meaningful role in overseeing or reviewing the quality of FOIA responses. On September 8, 2015, Secretary Kerry announced the appointment of a new Transparency Coordinator, charged with improving document preservation and transparency systems.[44] This is a positive step, but the following areas, in addition to the lack of compliance with legal and regulatory requirements, need immediate attention:

Lack of Written Policies and Procedures: Although other Department components, such as the Bureaus of Diplomatic Security and International Narcotics and Law Enforcement Affairs, have their own written FOIA guidance or standard operating procedures, S/ES does not. S/ES does use guides on how to search its own databases, EVEREST and STARS, but these are not FOIA specific and no criteria for conducting database searches have been developed. The FOIA Analyst for S/ES reported learning how to perform a FOIA search from on-the-job training. *Standards for Internal Control in the Federal Government* emphasizes the importance of documenting policies and procedures to provide a reasonable assurance that activities comply with applicable laws and regulations.[45] Written policies and procedures are also important for continuity because they increase the likelihood that, when organizational changes occur, institutional knowledge is shared with new staff.[46] Other agencies have recommended written policies and procedures as a best practice. For example, the Office of Inspector General for the Environmental Protection Agency recommends that all regional and program offices responsible for FOIA responses adopt written standard operating procedures to ensure quality control.[47] The Office of Inspector General for the Department of Energy has made a similar recommendation, noting, "without formalized policy and procedures, it could be difficult for an individual unfamiliar with the process to take an active role in filling FOIA requests, possibly leading to delays or inefficiencies in responding to requests."[48]

Inconsistent S/ES Monitoring Efforts: *Standards for Internal Control in the Federal Government* also emphasizes the importance of ongoing monitoring that is built into an entity's operations. Other agencies' monitoring activities vary widely. At some agencies, senior attorneys or career members of the Senior Executive Service are responsible for approving FOIA responses; at others, administrative staff handle the entire FOIA search and review process.[49] Nonetheless, standards emphasize that monitoring should include regular management and supervisory

---

[44] U.S. Department of State Press Statement, *Transparency Coordinator* (Sept. 8, 2015), available at http://www.state.gov/secretary/remarks/2015/09/246691.htm.

[45] GAO-14-704G.

[46] *See, e.g.,* GAO, *Social Security Disability: Management Controls Needed to Strengthen Demonstration Projects* (GAO-08-1053, September 2008).

[47] EPA, Office of Inspector General, *EPA Has Improved Its Response to Freedom of Information Act Requests But Further Improvement Is Needed* (09-P-0127, March 2009).

[48] DOE, Office of Inspector General, *Department's Freedom of Information Act Request Process* (OAS-SR-10-03, Sept. 2010).

[49] *See, e.g.,* Nuclear Regulatory Commission, Office of Inspector General, *Evaluation of Involvement of Political Appointees in NRC's FOIA Process* (OIG-15-A-18, August 2015) and Social Security Administration, Office of the Inspector General, *Freedom of Information Act Response Process* (A-03-15-50107, August 2015).

---

activities, comparisons, reconciliations, and other routine actions.[50] Such actions may include assessing employee performance with FOIA compliance, conducting spot checks, and establishing and reviewing metrics. Performance standards within S/ES for handling FOIA matters are incomplete. In 2012, OIG recommended that the Department place responsibility at all stages of the process and update performance standards, position descriptions, and work commitments to reflect FOIA responsibilities.[51] While the Deputy Director's performance standards have consistently contained multiple references to that individual's responsibilities as FOIA coordinator, the performance standards for the Deputy Director's former supervisors[52] in the Director of Secretariat Staff position have not mentioned FOIA at all.

Other oversight activities have also been inconsistent. The Deputy Director reviews the FOIA Analyst's search and the records identified. However, the past two Directors of Secretariat Staff reported minimal involvement in the FOIA process, other than providing occasional briefings to supervisors on high-profile or sensitive requests. The past two Directors did not review actual FOIA searches and responses, even on a spot-check basis, for quality, timeliness, thoroughness, or consistency. They also did not gather or review any metrics or other tracking information on S/ES FOIA activities. The current Director, who has been in the position since July 2015, told OIG that, while she periodically reviews FOIA responses, depending on the scope and nature of the FOIA request, she does not carry out any spot checks for accuracy. The current Director also reviews status reports that contain basic information on the date of the request and the offices tasked with conducting searches. No one in S/ES reviews the methodology of FOIA searches tasked to the other components in the Office of the Secretary (S, D, P and C).

Limited IPS Review Capability: The FAM designates IPS as responsible for the Department's compliance with FOIA,[53] and Department guidance specifically requires IPS to ensure that responses are timely, accurate, and complete.[54] However, IPS is almost completely dependent on FOIA coordinators in individual bureaus and offices to ensure that search results meet FOIA requirements. IPS does not have the ability to do independent spot checks in part because it does not have access to the unique databases used to conduct the searches, such as the EVEREST system used by the Office of the Secretary. According to IPS, the quality of responses to requests for FOIA searches varies across the Department. For example, IPS reported that the form documenting the search result (Form DS-1748) the FOIA coordinators submit is sometimes missing key information, such as the files searched and the search terms used. If this information is missing or if IPS identifies another inconsistency, it may ask for a search to be redone. IPS reported that its reviewers have at times spent weeks working with FOIA coordinators to obtain complete responses. In some cases, IPS will contact the FOIA coordinator's supervisor or executive-level staff within the office to resolve an issue. IPS's engagement with S/ES has been

---

[50] GAO-14-704G, at §§ 16.04, 16.05.

[51] The Department agreed with these recommendations but has yet to take action.

[52] The performance standards for the current Director of Secretariat Staff were not yet available for review at the close of OIG's work.

[53] 1 FAM 214.2.

[54] U.S. Department of State, *FOIA Guidance For State Department Employees* (2010).

limited, with its only contact typically being the Deputy Director. IPS also reports that it has contacted L attorneys for assistance when it has had difficulty obtaining complete responses from S/ES. In one case regarding a request for emails, correspondence, memos, internal notes, and other pertinent documents and records relating to a former S staff member, IPS tasked S/ES with a search in November 2013, but S/ES did not complete the search until December 2014 after the involvement of L. One L attorney characterized routine S/ES searches as frequently deficient, except in instances when FOIA litigation has commenced.

Insufficient Training: During OIG's 2012 inspection of A/GIS, IPS reported to OIG that most Department employees are poorly informed about FOIA principles and procedures, as well as about the importance of providing information to the public. IPS has since provided two Department-wide annual training courses on FOIA, recordkeeping, and classification issues. Records maintained by IPS show that no more than two S/ES employees have attended trainings, open houses, or workshops offered by IPS, and no one from S, D, P, or C has attended.[55] In addition to the annual training sessions, IPS has trained specific offices on FOIA at their request. Twelve bureaus, offices, or embassies have requested and completed this training since 2014, but S/ES is not among them.

S/ES FOIA Searches and Responses Are Sometimes Inaccurate and Incomplete

These procedural weaknesses, coupled with the lack of oversight by leadership and failure to routinely search emails, appear to contribute to inaccurate and incomplete responses. L attorneys and officials in IPS recalled several instances when S/ES searches have yielded inaccurate or incomplete results, though they were unable to determine the magnitude of this problem. The attorneys also noted that FOIA requesters have been able to produce evidence of the existence of records responsive to a FOIA request despite the attestation by S/ES that no responsive records existed.[56]

S/ES has not taken any corrective actions to ensure the accuracy and completeness of FOIA searches. *Standards for Internal Control in the Federal Government* notes that management should remediate identified deficiencies in controls and determine appropriate corrective actions on a timely basis.[57] Implementing such corrective actions could protect the Department from sanctions. For example, in litigated cases, incomplete searches by S/ES can expose the Department to financial liability, including attorney fees and other litigation costs.[58] The Department and its leadership could also be subject to contempt citations if they were found to

---

[55] According to S/ES, the FOIA Analyst also attended workshops at the Department of Justice.

[56] Department attorneys noted that these instances do not necessarily indicate that the search for records was inadequate. Not all documents created by the Department are Federal records. It is also possible that a document existed at one time but was subsequently destroyed either in compliance with the records disposition schedules or because of poor recordkeeping practices.

[57] GAO-14-704G, at §§ 17.01, 17.05.

[58] 5 U.S.C. § 552(a)(4)(E).

have violated rules requiring candor to the court.[59] Although L attorneys are not aware of an instance where such sanctions were imposed, it is not uncommon for courts to order the Department to conduct additional searches or provide additional information explaining the adequacy of the searches conducted.[60]

OIG has been unable to determine the extent of these inaccuracies, but recent examples of incomplete searches and responses to FOIA queries involving the Office of the Secretary include the following:

- In March 2010, the Associated Press (AP) filed a FOIA request for copies of all of former Secretary Clinton's public and private calendars and schedules. IPS tasked S/ES with searching for responsive records. In November 2010, S/ES provided IPS with records that were non-responsive. IPS then contacted the Office of the Secretary directly and also contacted L for guidance. IPS has no record of receiving responses and the FOIA request sat dormant for several years. In August 2013, AP resubmitted its FOIA request and updated it to include a request for all of the calendars from Secretary Clinton's tenure. In June 2014, December 2014, and again in July 2015, S/ES provided IPS with information regarding the location of these records, which had been retired. In March 2015, after failing to receive responses to multiple FOIA requests, AP filed suit against the Department.[61] In a July 2015 court filing, the Department disclosed that it had finally conducted a search and located at least 4,440 paper and electronic records related to Secretary Clinton's calendars and schedules, which were created by various personnel in the Office of the Secretary.

- In December 2012, the nonprofit organization Citizens for Responsibility and Ethics in Washington (CREW) sent a FOIA request to the Department seeking records "sufficient to show the number of email accounts of, or associated with, Secretary Hillary Rodham Clinton, and the extent to which those email accounts are identifiable as those of or associated with Secretary Clinton."[62] On May 10, 2013, IPS replied to CREW, stating that "no records responsive to your request were located."[63] At the time the request was

---

[59] *See, e.g., Judicial Watch v. Internal Revenue Service*, Civil Action No. 13-1559 (D.D.C.), where contempt of court citations have been threatened against the IRS in a FOIA lawsuit.

[60] *See e.g., Tarzia v. Clinton*, Civil Action No. 1:10-cv-05654-FM (S.D.N.Y. January 30, 2012); *Beltranena v. Clinton*, Civil Action No. 1:09-cv-01457-BJR (D.D.C. March 17, 2011).

[61] *The Associated Press v. U.S Dept. of State*, Civil Action No. 1:15-cv-00345-RJL (D.D.C.).

[62] Later in the letter as part of its request to waive processing fees, CREW stated its belief that the records it was requesting were "likely to contribute to greater public awareness of the extent to which Secretary Clinton, like the administrator of the Environmental Protection Agency (EPA), use[s] email accounts not readily identifiable as her accounts." CREW also noted: "[r]ecently it was reported that [EPA] Administrator Jackson established alias email accounts to conduct official government business, including an account under the name 'Richard Windson' which is not publicly attributable to her. . . Through this FOIA, CREW seeks to learn how widespread this practice is, and to evaluate the extent to which it has led to under-inclusive responses to FOIA, discovery, and congressional requests, and a failure to preserve records in a way that complies with the Federal Records Act."

[63] The response also noted:

received, dozens of senior officials throughout the Department, including members of Secretary Clinton's immediate staff, exchanged emails with the Secretary using the personal accounts she used to conduct official business. OIG found evidence that the Secretary's then-Chief of Staff was informed of the request at the time it was received and subsequently tasked staff to follow up. However, OIG found no evidence to indicate that any of these senior officials reviewed the search results or approved the response to CREW. OIG also found no evidence that the S/ES, L, and IPS staff involved in responding to requests for information, searching for records, or drafting the response had knowledge of the Secretary's email usage. [64] Furthermore, it does not appear that S/ES searched any email records, even though the request clearly encompassed emails. [65]

- In May 2013, the nonprofit organization Judicial Watch filed a FOIA request for records related to the authorization of a former adviser to Secretary Clinton to undertake employment outside the Department. IPS tasked S/ES with performing the search, which returned 23 documents. In August 2013, AP filed a FOIA request seeking the same information, but S/ES only returned five documents for a nearly identical request.

- In May 2014, Judicial Watch filed a FOIA request seeking records related to talking points given to Ambassador to the United Nations Susan Rice concerning the September 11, 2012, attack on the U.S. diplomatic facilities in Benghazi, Libya. In July 2014, Judicial Watch filed suit in district court because the Department had not responded to the request. In September 2014, IPS tasked S/ES with conducting the search. S/ES initially identified five documents but only returned four documents to IPS because it did not view the fifth document, an email, as responsive. IPS provided the four documents to Judicial Watch in November 2014. In June 2015, pursuant to an earlier request, several former officials provided the Department with copies of records that were in their possession. One of these records included the fifth document identified in the September 2014 search by S/ES as part of a longer email chain. S/ES reviewed this

---

It may be helpful for you to know that messages from the Secretary are occasionally transmitted to the Department via email. However, these messages are transmitted from a "dummy" email address that is not capable of receiving replies, rather than from a functioning email account.

[64] On August 11, 2014, the Department produced to the House Select Committee on Benghazi documents related to the 2012 attack on U.S. facilities in Benghazi. The production included a number of emails revealing that Secretary Clinton used a personal email account to conduct official business. OIG discovered four instances, between July and September 2014, in which staff from L, A, or the Bureau of Legislative Affairs reviewed the CREW request and the Department's May 2013 response, but the Department did not amend its response. L and A staff also told OIG that the Department does not customarily revise responses to closed FOIA requests. Nevertheless, during the course of this review, Department staff advised OIG of their belief that the Department's response to CREW was incorrect and that it should have been revised to include the former Secretary's personal email account used to conduct official government business. OIG notes that the issue may have been resolved insofar as the Department is now engaged in the process of publishing on its FOIA website the 55,000 pages of personal emails produced by Secretary Clinton.

[65] According to a February 26, 2013, memorandum to IPS, S/ES stated that its FOIA Analyst spent an hour searching through the Department cable and telegram system and STARS and did not discover any responsive records. The Deputy Director reviewed the search and results, but no other official within S/ES conducted a review.

---

document and determined that it was in fact responsive to the FOIA request, which the Department disclosed to the court in July 2015.

RECOMMENDATIONS

To ensure that FOIA requests involving the Office of the Secretary generate timely, accurate, and complete searches and responses, OIG has issued the following recommendations to the Bureau of Administration, the Office of the Secretary, and the Department's Transparency Coordinator. Their responses can be found in Appendix A.

Recommendation 1: The Bureau of Administration should identify necessary permanent personnel as part of FOIA workforce planning efforts and quickly acquire those resources so the Department can comply with applicable law and improve the timeliness of FOIA searches and responses.

Management Response: In its November 30, 2015, response, the Bureau of Administration concurred with this recommendation. It noted that its fiscal year 2017 budget request includes funding for two additional permanent positions for FOIA and continued funding of 50 temporary positions (eligible family members and rehired annuitants).

OIG Reply: OIG considers the recommendation resolved. The recommendation can be closed when OIG receives and accepts documentation showing that these 52 positions have been filled. However, OIG strongly encourages the Bureau of Administration to continue to monitor its staffing levels to determine whether additional permanent personnel are needed to process FOIA requests.

Recommendation 2: The Office of the Secretary, Executive Secretariat, should fully comply with FOIA requirements and Department guidance by (a) searching email records for all FOIA requests in which relevant records are likely maintained in email accounts; and (b) reminding S/ES employees that Federal records contained in personal emails may be subject to FOIA when in the Department's control and should be preserved in the Department's recordkeeping systems.

Management Response: In its November 30, 2015, response, the Executive Secretariat concurred with this recommendation. It noted that its current practice is to search email records for all FOIA requests in which responsive records are likely to be located.

OIG Reply: OIG considers the recommendation resolved. This recommendation can be closed when OIG receives a copy of S/ES FOIA policies and procedures that require a search of email records for all FOIA requests in which relevant records are likely maintained in email accounts and a reminder to S/ES employees that Federal records contained in personal email may be subject to FOIA and must be preserved in the Department's recordkeeping systems.

Recommendation 3: The Office of the Secretary, Executive Secretariat should address weaknesses in its FOIA processes by:

- Developing written policies and procedures for performing FOIA searches addressed to the Office of the Secretary.
- Including FOIA duties as part of the performance standards for the Director of Secretariat Staff.
- Ensuring that executive-level staff members rigorously oversee the FOIA process, to include regular monitoring activities and implementing corrective actions as needed.
- Coordinating FOIA training for all S/ES, Office of the Secretary, Deputy Secretaries, Under Secretary for Political Affairs, and Counselor of the Department staff.

Management Response: In its November 30, 2015, response, the Executive Secretariat concurred with this recommendation. It noted that S/ES is currently drafting FOIA policies and procedures and metrics for timeliness and completeness of FOIA responses. S/ES also noted that the work requirements for the current Director of the Executive Secretariat include FOIA responsibilities and that FOIA training for S/ES staff is in progress.

OIG Reply: OIG considers the recommendation resolved. This recommendation can be closed when OIG receives copies of S/ES FOIA policies and procedures that include monitoring activities and the development of metrics that are reviewed by executive-level staff; a copy of the work requirements for the current Director that include FOIA responsibilities; and FOIA training records for S/ES employees.

Recommendation 4: The Department's Transparency Coordinator should work with IPS to develop a quality assurance plan to identify and address Department-wide vulnerabilities in the FOIA process, including lack of monitoring of FOIA searches and responses, technological challenges, and the sufficiency of staffing and training.

Management Response: In her response, the Transparency Coordinator concurred with this recommendation. She endorsed an accountability framework for the Department that includes processes, roles, standards, and metrics to help ensure that important legal, administrative, evidential, and historical information requirements of the Department are met.

OIG Reply: OIG considers the recommendation resolved. This recommendation can be closed when OIG receives a copy of the quality assurance plan.

APPENDIX A: MANAGEMENT RESPONSES

United States Department of State

Assistant Secretary of State
for Administration
Washington, D.C. 20520

November 30, 2015

<u>UNCLASSIFIED</u>

TO: Inspector General - Steve Linick

FROM: Bureau of Administration - Joyce A. Barr

SUBJECT: Draft report - Review of the Department of State's FOIA
             Processes for Requests Involving the Office of the Secretary
             (ESP-16-01 dated November 13, 2015)

The Bureau of Administration thanks the OIG for the opportunity to respond to the subject draft report and provides the following in response to the single recommendation for this bureau's action.

Recommendation 1: The Bureau of Administration should identify necessary permanent personnel as part of the FOIA workforce planning efforts and quickly acquire those resources so the Department can comply with applicable law and improve the timeliness of FOIA searches and responses.

The Bureau of Administration concurs with this recommendation. As the OIG is aware, increasing the number of A/GIS/IPS FOIA staff is one part of the solution for improving Department response time to FOIA cases that are often broad and extremely complex. To date, A Bureau has taken the following steps to increase our FOIA staffing/resources in Fiscal Year 2016 and our request for Fiscal Year 2017.

The A/GIS approved budget request for FY 2016, which includes FOIA, was $13,932,000. The A Bureau recently requested an additional $8.3M for FY 2016 to cover the cost of salaries, support, information technology (IT), and other necessities for 50 new positions dedicated to FOIA operations ("FOIA 50"). Hiring is currently under way for 10 Eligible Family Members (EFMs) and 40 subject matter expert Foreign Service annuitants. A minimum Top Secret

<u>UNCLASSIFIED</u>

-2-

clearance is required for each of these positions and hiring eligible family members and annuitants helps to expedite that clearance requirement. The FY 2016 funding level for these activities is subject to the availability of FY 2016 appropriations which are currently pending with Congress.

A Bureau's FY 2017 request to OMB includes two FTE and additional support costs including resources to improve FOIA systems. It is our understanding the OMB pass-back for FY 2017 is expected later this week. If provided, the resources requested for FY 2017 should allow the A Bureau to fund, at least partially, the recurring costs to maintain the FOIA 50 positions in FY 2017 (i.e. salaries, support, IT, etc.).

The A Bureau appreciates the OIG's support of our ongoing efforts to improve the Department's FOIA program.

UNCLASSIFIED

United States Department of State

Washington, D.C. 20520

November 30, 2015

<u>UNCLASSIFIED</u>

TO: Steve Linick, Inspector General

FROM: MaryKary Carlson, Acting Executive Secretary

SUBJECT: Response to Draft OIG Review of the Department of State's
              FOIA Processes for Requests Involving the Office of the
              Secretary

The Executive Secretariat thanks the OIG for the opportunity to respond to this review and values the OIG's study of the Department's FOIA process. The Secretariat has the following specific responses to the recommendations contained in the report.

Recommendation 1: While this recommendation is directed to the A Bureau, the Executive Secretariat notes that it has experienced a commensurate increase in the number of FOIA requests and also needs more staff dedicated to FOIA-related work. S/ES-S is currently in the process of reprogramming one FTE position to work on FOIA. While the growing FOIA workload has affected response times, S/ES-S records do not match the number of pending FOIA requests cited in the draft report. S/ES-S and A/GIS/IPS have agreed to work together to review and reconcile the number of outstanding FOIA cases involving the Office of the Secretary.

Recommendation 2: The Executive Secretariat strongly agrees with the OIG recommendation that it should fully comply with FOIA requirements and Department guidance by searching email records for all FOIA requests in which relevant records are likely maintained in email accounts. This is the current practice of the Executive Secretariat staff (S/ES-S) and is the instruction provided to all offices engaged in FOIA searches involving the Office of the Secretary and comports with the instruction provided to all offices in the Department.

The Executive Secretariat further agrees with the OIG recommendation that S/ES employees should be reminded that Federal records contained in personal emails may be subject to FOIA and should be preserved in the Department's record-keeping systems. All Department employees received this guidance and

- 2 -

instruction from the Under Secretary for Management on October 17, 2014 and it is reiterated to all S/ES and S bureau employees in their check-in, periodic training, and check-out briefings on records management. As instructed in the above-referenced guidance from the Under Secretary for Management, to ensure Federal records contained in personal emails are preserved in the Department's recordkeeping systems, all employees are required to copy or forward any personal message containing a Federal record to their official Department email accounts for appropriate retention and archiving.

Recommendation 3: The Executive Secretariat welcomes the OIG's suggestions for improvement in its FOIA processes and concurs with all four elements of the recommendation. The Executive Secretariat has already taken steps to implement these recommendations, specifically:

1. Written policies and procedures (SOPs) are currently being drafted for all involved in the FOIA search process in the S bureau. These SOPs will be cleared with A/GIS/IPS and others in the Department, as appropriate.
2. The work requirements of the current Director of the Executive Secretariat Staff (S/ES-S) include oversight and management of the FOIA process for S/ES.
3. The Director of the Executive Secretariat Staff oversees all FOIA searches conducted by S/ES-S staff and reviews and approves all responses to A Bureau. S/ES-S management is developing metrics for timeliness of response and completeness of searches.
4. The Acting Executive Secretary and other senior Executive Secretariat managers have recently completed FOIA training conducted by A/GIS, and training sessions are being arranged for staff of the office of the Secretary, the Deputy Secretaries, the Under Secretary for Political Affairs, and the Counselor.

The Secretariat notes (p. 9 of draft report) the OIG comment on the fact that S/ES tasks current S, D, D-MR, P, and C employees to search through their own email accounts for responsive records in FOIA cases. The Executive Secretariat would like to clarify for OIG that this is standard practice Department-wide per guidance from A Bureau. The Executive Secretariat would further like to clarify for OIG that S/ES-S does review the results of all such searches.

Recommendation 4: The Executive Secretariat looks forward to continuing ongoing collaboration with the Transparency Coordinator to improve the FOIA process. In particular, the Secretariat strongly supports the recommendation to focus on technological challenges to conducting successful FOIA searches.

TO: Steve Linick, Inspector General

FROM: Janice L. Jacobs, Transparency Coordinator

SUBJECT: Response to Draft OIG Review of the Department of State's
               FOIA Processes for Requests Involving the Office of the
               Secretary

I appreciate the work by your Special Projects team to identify needed
improvements to processes and procedures related to the Department's handling of
requests under the Freedom of Information Act (FOIA). I will take the opportunity
in the Quality Assurance Plan (QAP) to address FOIA-related issues
(Recommendation 4) within the context of information management within the
Department.

As Transparency Coordinator, my overall vision is a 21st century enterprise-wide
information management system that advances the Department's goals of increased
efficiency, transparency, and accountability. Under this vision, records
management is less an independent arm in the information landscape and a more
integrated process and functional system within a whole-of-enterprise information
and knowledge management environment.

Information is one of the Department's most valuable assets requiring careful
management, thoughtful governance and strategic consideration in its use and
control. The IG report recommends a stronger focus on information governance,
technological challenges and sufficient staffing and training. Specifically, the
Department needs an accountability framework that covers the processes, roles,
standards, and metrics to help ensure that important legal, administrative,
evidential and historical information requirements of the Department are met.
Creating this framework is the goal of the QAP I will prepare, in concert with
A/GIS/IPS, S/ES and other pertinent offices.

The Department is not alone in dealing with the information management
challenges associated with today's fast changing, data-driven world. Many
agencies have the same issues: records management/FOIA traditionally have not
been a high priority; a new norm of a high volume of requests and litigation cases;
staffing and funding shortfalls; outdated technology or technology silos;
insufficient records-related internal controls; and insufficient training/education on

the importance of effective management of information/records. Secretary Kerry recognizes these challenges and my appointment was one step towards trying to address these matters holistically.

My plan will address all these issues, again with a view towards finding Department-wide solutions. I will start with a communications strategy that begins to talk about information management in new ways to highlight the important role that all Department employees play in preserving records. This will begin with a message from the top followed up by periodic messages to domestic and overseas employees.

Thank you for the opportunity to provide comments to the report on FOIA-related processes. I look forward to helping to implement your recommendations both on FOIA and on records preservation in general.

ABBREVIATIONS

A	Bureau of Administration
A/GIS	Office of Global Information Services
AP	Associated Press
C	Counselor of the Department
CREW	Citizens for Responsibility and Ethics in Washington
D	Deputy Secretary
Department	Department of State
Deputy Director	S/ES Deputy Director of Correspondence, Records, and Staffing
FAM	*Foreign Affairs Manual*
FOIA	Freedom of Information Act
GAO	Government Accountability Office
IPS	Office of Information Programs and Services
FREEDOMS	Freedom of Information Document Management System
L	Office of the Legal Adviser
OIG	Office of Inspector General
P	Under Secretary for Political Affairs
S	Office of the Secretary
S/ES	Office of the Secretary, Executive Secretariat
S/ES-IRM	S/ES Office of Information Resources Management
STARS	Secretariat Tracking and Retrieval System

OIG EVALUATIONS AND SPECIAL PROJECTS TEAM

Jennifer L. Costello, Team Leader
David Z. Seide, Team Leader

Michael Bosserdet, Office of Inspections
Kelly Minghella, Office of Investigations
Brett Fegley, Office of Inspections
Aaron Leonard, Office of Audits
Robert Lovely, Office of Evaluations and Special Projects
Jeffrey McDermott, Office of Evaluations and Special Projects
Kristene McMinn, Office of Inspections
Eric Myers, Office of Investigations
Phillip Ropella, Office of Audits
Timothy Williams, Office of Inspections